Living Waters that Heal

David Hurst

Table of Contents

Dedication

First and foremost, I want to express my gratitude to my God, my Lord, and my friend, Jesus Christ. Without Him, I would not be where I am today. He has guided, protected, and sustained me throughout my life.

I also want to thank my wife, Brittany Hurst. She is an incredible woman who has grown alongside me during our 13 years of marriage. She is a wonderful mother to our three children.

I owe a debt of gratitude to my parents, Pamela and David Hurst Sr., who raised me well and instilled in me the values I hold dear.

A special thanks to my pastors, Daron and Joy Hudspeth, the shepherds of Life Church in St. Petersburg, FL. Their sound doctrine, wisdom in navigating life's challenges, and genuine love for people have been a blessing to us all.

Finally, to my prison ministry team, you are an amazing group of individuals. I admire your dedication and commitment to reaching the lost. Your passion inspires me every day.

Thank you all!

Introduction

I pray this book finds you well. It was born out of my preaching and speaking on this topic as the Holy Spirit has led me, whether in correctional facilities, or various meetings. For some time, the Holy Spirit has been dealing with me about true healing and deliverance, which many of us need. Too often, as believers, we struggle with past issues or challenges in our current walk, even after we've been saved.

Many of these struggles are deep wounds and scars that we try to hide, presenting a false narrative of a picture perfect life. We resist vulnerability and the loss of control over our situations. During my studies on holiness and walking with God, I've realized that while we may appear outwardly polished, our inner selves can be suffering from depression, anxiety, hatred, perversion, pride, gluttony, fear, and more.

As you read this book, I encourage you to reflect on the hidden areas where you desire God's hand to intervene. I cannot cover every specific topic or situation because each of our lives presents unique circumstances known only to God, who can truly help us. My hope is that this book inspires you to seek the Holy Spirit and allows healing to take place in your life.

Reflecting on the story of creation, we witness the transition from chaos to order. In Genesis, God created the heavens and the earth, and the earth was without form and void, with darkness over the deep—an image of chaos. I firmly believe in what's called the gap theory, which suggests a gap between Genesis 1:1 and 1:2. I don't believe our God creates in chaos; rather, He can bring order out of chaos.

We begin to see the Spirit of God moving upon the waters. This is what happens in our lives—the Spirit moves, and God speaks light into our situations, bringing organization and clarity. Salvation is just the beginning; there should be a continuous flow of order and new beginnings in our lives through the Spirit of God.

I pray this book guides us deeper into the Spirit, enabling God to work in our lives so that we can be prayerfully healed and delivered.

David Hurst

The Outpour

What is Spirit Baptism? Some of you may already know from personal experience, others may have heard about it from different denominations and may deny its need, claiming they received everything when they said a prayer. Some may have never heard of it or been taught about it, while others might feel uncomfortable with the idea of speaking in tongues as the initial evidence, believing it's something that was done away with.

Baptism means full immersion, often referring to water baptism. However, in the context of Scripture, it also applies to the Baptism of the Holy Ghost, which entails full immersion in the Spirit.

No matter where you stand on this, I hope you approach this discussion with an open and prayerful heart and mind. As a Pentecostal man, I do not discount anyone's walk with God, as I believe that everything from belief to Spirit baptism is a work of the Holy Spirit. There is a wealth of material to study on the topic of Spirit Baptism, including books like *Speaking in Tongues* by Robert P. Menzies, *Essentials of Pentecostal Theology* by Tony Richie, *The New Birth* by David K. Bernard, *Initial Evidence* by Gary B. McGee, and *Power* by Nichol Collins. These references come from various Pentecostal traditions, including Apostolic Pentecostals, Assemblies of God, and Church of God.

Spirit baptism is a true biblical experience that continues today. I do not believe in making up gibberish or being taught what to say. It's a genuine experience like the one in Acts 2:4, where the Spirit gave the utterance and people spoke in other languages. The book of Acts spans over 30 years, covering many of the epistles, and when you study it, you'll see references to various churches and the events that took place. Luke, the author of Acts, provides the details necessary to understand what is happening. In his Gospel, Luke talks more than anyone else about the Spirit of God or being filled with the Holy Ghost.

As we go through this chapter, the focus will be on Spirit Baptism biblically to give us a clearer understanding.

The Spirit Baptism in the Bible: Baptism in the Holy Ghost is mentioned throughout the New Testament, with foreshadowing in the Old Testament. In John 1:33, John the Baptist speaks of Jesus as the one who will baptize with the Holy Ghost. The gospels of Mark, Matthew, and Luke also speak of Jesus baptizing with the Holy Ghost and fire (Matthew 3:11, Mark 1:8, Luke 3:16). Jesus reiterates this in Acts 1:5, right before Pentecost, after His resurrection. The word "with" in Acts 1:5 can be understood as "in," so it can be said that they were baptized *in* the Holy Ghost.

Moving on to Acts 1:8, we can better understand Spirit Baptism as we journey through the book of Acts and connect it with Old Testament typology.

Acts 1:8 states: 'But ye shall receive power **after** that the Holy Ghost is come upon you: and ye shall be witnesses unto me both in Jerusalem, and in all Judaea, and in Samaria, and unto the uttermost part of the earth." Compare this with Luke 24:48-49, where it is said that the disciples are witnesses of these things, and that the promise of the Father would be sent to them. This was meant to be an outpouring of the Spirit upon the disciples and all true believers. As Jesus said in John 14:18, "I will come to you," indicating that the Spirit would be available to all believers and empower them for greater works than even Jesus had done.

But how can we do greater works than Jesus, who is God manifest in the flesh? The answer lies in the scope of His ministry. Jesus' earthly ministry was primarily confined to Israel, while we, as His followers, are called to be witnesses to the entire world. Through the empowerment of the Holy Spirit, we are equipped to reach people across the globe, extending the message of Christ and His works to every corner of the earth.

In essence, "greater works" does not imply that believers will do more miraculous deeds than Jesus, but that the scope of His work would expand and multiply through His followers empowered by the Holy Spirit, impacting the world on a global scale.

Greater Reach: Jesus' ministry was primarily confined to the region of Israel. His followers, empowered by the Holy Spirit, are called to spread His message to the entire world. The "greater works" could refer to the global outreach of the gospel that His disciples would carry out after His resurrection, especially through the church's mission to the nations.

The Holy Spirit's Empowerment: Jesus' followers would receive the Holy Spirit after His ascension (Acts 1:8). The Spirit would empower believers to do works of healing, miracles, preaching, and evangelism that Jesus did during His ministry. But these works would be done not by their own power but by the power of the Spirit within them.

Continuing Jesus' Work: The "greater works" don't necessarily mean that the miracles or deeds performed by believers would be *greater* in quality than those of Jesus. Instead, it points to the *continuation* and expansion of His work.

Believers, through the power of the Holy Spirit, would continue His work of healing, teaching, and saving, reaching more people and territories than Jesus did in His lifetime.

Greater Impact: Jesus' death, resurrection, and ascension opened the way for salvation to all people. Believers, empowered by the Holy Spirit, have the opportunity to impact more lives in a way that Jesus' physical ministry on earth could not. The "greater works" could include spreading the message of the gospel across the world, leading to the transformation of countless lives.

So, the question I ask many believers is, what do you have to lose with Spirit Baptism? I would say: nothing, and you have "much to gain."

1 Corinthians 12:13 says we are baptized into one body and drink from one Spirit. Let's continue through Acts to explore further examples of Spirit Baptism.

Acts 2: The Day of Pentecost- The first significant account of Spirit Baptism occurs in Acts 2. When the day of Pentecost was fully come, there was a sound of a rushing mighty wind, cloven tongues of fire, and they were filled with the Holy Ghost and began to speak in other tongues as the Spirit gave them utterance.

The word "fully" and "filled" appear multiple times in the first four verses of Acts 2. The word "fully" means "to fill completely," while "filled" means "to make full or complete." This fullness is important because what happened in Acts 2 was not just a momentary event but the beginning of a lasting, complete experience of the Holy Spirit.

Pentecost, or the Feast of Weeks, comes 50 days after Passover. Passover required unleavened bread, but Pentecost, being a harvest feast, required two loaves of fine flour. This feast represents the filling that occurs when we hear the Gospel, believe, repent, and are baptized in Jesus' name. We are then filled with the Gift of the Holy Ghost. This shows that there is no distinction between Jew and Gentile, as the Apostle Paul later emphasizes in his epistles.

In verse 10, we see proselytes (Gentiles who converted to Judaism) being part of God's plan, indicating that Pentecost was not just for the Jews but for all people.

In Acts 2:11, the crowd called the experience the "wonderful works of God." Throughout Acts, we see many other instances of being filled or full of the Holy Ghost (Acts 2:4, 4:8, 4:31, 9:17, 13:9, 13:52).

This experience is meant to be more than just a one-time event; it should be a continual walk with God, as we will explore further in this discussion.

Acts 8: Belief vs. Spirit Baptism- In Acts 8:4-19, Philip preaches in Samaria, and many believe and are baptized in Jesus' name. However, verses 15-16 tell us that the Holy Ghost had not yet fallen upon them. This shows that belief and baptism in Jesus' name are not the same as receiving the Holy Ghost. Peter and John then lay hands on the people, and they receive the Holy Ghost.

The question arises: how did they know they received the Holy Ghost? Based on Acts 2 and the other accounts, it's clear that the evidence was speaking in tongues. Simon, who witnessed this, was so amazed that he wanted to buy the ability to give the Holy Ghost to others.

Acts 10: Gentiles- In Acts 10, we see the Gentile Pentecost. Cornelius, a devout man, receives the Holy Ghost, and Peter preaches to him about the death, burial, and resurrection of Jesus. In verses 44-48, the Holy Ghost falls on all who heard the word, and they speak in tongues, just as the apostles had in Acts 2. Peter refers to this event in Acts 11:14, noting that the Holy Ghost fell upon them as it had at the beginning, during Pentecost.

Acts 19: Ephesian Disciples- Finally, in Acts 19, Paul encounters a group of believers and asks them, "Have you received the Holy Ghost since you believed?" This shows that there is a difference between believing and receiving the Holy Ghost. After they are baptized in Jesus' name, the Holy Ghost comes upon them, and they speak in tongues and prophesy (Acts 19:6).

This shows that Spirit Baptism is not only an immersion in the Holy Spirit but an active, transformative experience, often evidenced by speaking in tongues, as seen throughout the book of Acts.

Spirit Baptism is a powerful, ongoing experience that equips believers to walk in the fullness of God's power and presence. From the Old Testament typologies to the clear teachings in the New Testament, it is evident that Spirit Baptism is an essential part of the believer's life. Whether you're new to the concept or have been taught differently, I encourage you to study these scriptures with an open heart and receive all that God has promised.

The Holy Ghost, when it comes upon people, represents the Spirit of God in action. In Scripture, we often see the Spirit of the Lord moving upon individuals or things. For example, Genesis 1:2 mentions the Spirit of God moving upon the waters. From this, we understand that the Spirit of God, or *Ruach* (which means "wind" or "breath"), is active and dynamic. The Holy Spirit is also referred to as *Ruach Hakodesh*, and this is what Jesus foretold would happen — the Spirit of God would fall upon them. In John 3:8, Jesus says that the wind blows where it wishes, and you hear its sound, illustrating the mysterious and active nature of the Holy Spirit.

The word "wind" here refers to the Holy Ghost or breath, while "sound" (from the Greek word *phone*, from which we get *phonics*) means "tone" or "voice." In the context of Spirit baptism in Acts, we might ask: what was the common sign when the Holy Ghost moved and filled those present? In **Genesis 1**, God moves over the formless earth, bringing order and life to a world once in chaos. His Spirit moved over the darkness and spoke light into existence. Similarly, God moves in our lives, bringing light to our darkness and breathing life into us.

There are several Old Testament examples that foreshadow the Baptism of the Holy Ghost, providing correlations that help us understand its significance.

Genesis 2:7 correlates with **John 20:22**, where God breathes into humanity, imparting life. This breath opens our eyes, hearts, and understanding to the word of God. I believe the Holy Ghost plays an active role in every aspect of a person's journey toward God. After Jesus breathed into His disciples, they gained a deeper understanding of the Scriptures. Then, when the Holy Ghost was poured out in Acts, that became the common experience for all believers.

The **Tower of Babel** in **Genesis 11** offers another insight: when God confused the languages of humanity, it was an act of division. However, in **Acts 2**, we see a unification through the speaking of tongues, as the Holy Spirit fills people and brings them together. This is echoed in **Zephaniah 3:9**, where God promises to restore a pure language, and His people will call on His name in one accord. This sounds very much like the fulfillment of the prophecy in Acts 2, as Peter explains, referencing the prophet Joel.

The **Law at Mount Sinai** in **Exodus** (50 days after the Exodus) has a parallel with **Pentecost**, which is 50 days after Passover. At Mount Sinai, the law was given on tablets of stone, but the first tablets were broken, symbolizing that the law was never meant to fulfill righteousness. The second set of tablets pointed to God's law being written on our hearts (as prophesied in **Ezekiel 36:26-28**, **Deuteronomy 6:6**, and **Jeremiah**

31:31-33). At both Mount Sinai and Pentecost, fire is present, and there is a meeting place for all people. However, some resisted or questioned. In both instances, God's presence brings transformation.

The **Elijah-Elisha** story is another powerful correlation. When Elijah ascended into heaven, his mantle (symbolizing God's Spirit) fell upon Elisha, giving him a double portion of Elijah's anointing. Similarly, when Jesus ascended into heaven, He left His mantle, the Holy Ghost (the Comforter), to fall upon His followers. This allows believers to do greater works, as Jesus promised, because through the Holy Spirit, we can be witnesses to the ends of the earth.

Lastly, in **Numbers 11:24-29**, two witnesses who were not in the tabernacle received the Spirit, leading Moses to declare that God would desire for His Spirit to rest upon all His people, and they would all be prophets. This shows God's desire for everyone to be filled with His Spirit, a promise that finds fulfillment in the New Testament through the baptism of the Holy Ghost.

Through these correlations, we see how the baptism of the Holy Ghost is not only a New Testament experience but a fulfillment of Old Testament promises and types. It is an active, life-giving force that brings believers into a deeper relationship with God and empowers them for His work.

Some may argue that all I need to do is confess with my mouth and believe in my heart, as stated in Romans 10:9, and they are good to go. However, let me clarify: when Paul wrote to the Romans, he was addressing believers who were already in the faith. He referred to them as saints (Romans 1:7), and their faith was well-known throughout the world (Romans 1:8). In Romans 1:12, Paul expressed a mutual faith with the Romans. Therefore, if Romans 10:9 is written to believers, the "salvation" Paul speaks of is not the initial salvation they received at conversion, but rather a future salvation—a heavenly home and a deeper, ongoing work of salvation (Romans 13:11).

As we conclude this chapter, I would be remiss if I didn't explain how one can biblically experience the fullness of salvation, including Spirit baptism.

Belief and Repentance: At the moment of belief and repentance, we recognize our need for a Savior. Repentance involves a death to the old self—a spiritual death, where something is subtracted from our lives. We turn away from our previous life and recognize our need for transformation.

Water Baptism in Jesus' Name: In water baptism, there is both subtraction and addition. We die to the old man, the "old Adam," and we are buried with Christ in baptism. As we are immersed in the water, we are symbolically buried with Jesus, and then, when we rise from the water, we are raised to new life in Christ. Through baptism, we identify with His death, burial, and resurrection (Romans 6:1-4, 1 Corinthians 15:3-4).

Spirit Baptism (Filling of the Holy Ghost): Spirit baptism is a divine experience where the breath of God fills us, the words of God come upon us, and a spiritual rebirth takes place.

Jesus declared, "I am the resurrection and the life" (John 11:25), and the Spirit's infilling is a part of that resurrection power.

Believe with faith: Look to Jesus and the cross as the source of your salvation (John 7:37-39).

Repentance: Truly renounce your old lifestyle and turn to God.

Ask: Remember, the Holy Spirit is a gift, not something to be begged for. Ask with faith, knowing it is freely given by God (Luke 11:13).

Be thirsty: Jesus promises that those who hunger and thirst for righteousness will be filled (Matthew 5:6). The Holy Spirit is likened to wells of water and rivers of living water.

Receive and Yield: Yield your unruly tongue and allow the Spirit to move within you. As the Spirit gives the utterance, speak in faith and allow the Spirit to fill you.

I encourage you to remain prayerful. Everything I've shared here is through the lens of how Christ describes the Spirit flowing like rivers of living water. This experience of the Holy Spirit is not just for those in the past, but for every believer today who seek to receive empowerment.

The Movement of His Presence

Now that we have a better understanding of the Baptism of the Holy Ghost and its experience, let's explore two books of the Bible that are essential for understanding the flow of the Spirit. While the entire Bible holds vital insights into pneumatology, the study of the Holy Spirit, we must especially recognize the role of the Holy Ghost in both the Old and New Testaments. In fact, Peter himself stated that the prophets of old spoke "as they were moved by the Holy Ghost" (2 Peter 1:21). The Bible is rich with references to the Holy Spirit, often using various titles and metaphors to describe His presence and activity.

In the Old Testament, the Holy Spirit is frequently referred to as the "Spirit of the Lord," and it is through the Scriptures that we see the Spirit at work in various ways. There are many references and symbols that help us understand the nature and work of the Holy Spirit. These symbols include fire, wind, breath, oil, and water, each revealing a unique aspect of His ministry and influence.

Some Key References to the Spirit of God in the Old Testament:

Genesis 1:2 – The Spirit of God is present at the creation of the world: "And the Spirit of God moved upon the face of the waters." This highlights the active role of the Holy Spirit in creation, bringing order and life to the formless earth.

Genesis 2:7 – God breathes life into man: "And the Lord God formed man of the dust of the ground, and breathed into his nostrils the breath of life; and man became a living soul." Here, the breath of life represents the Spirit's vitalizing power, making humanity spiritually alive.

Genesis 6:3 – The Spirit of God will not always strive with humanity: "And the Lord said, My spirit shall not always strive with man." This is a warning of the eventual withdrawal of the Holy Spirit's influence when humanity rejects God.

Exodus 31:1-5 – The Spirit empowers individuals to complete specific tasks: "See, I have called by name Bezaleel... and I have filled him with the Spirit of God, in wisdom, and in understanding, and in knowledge, and in all manner of workmanship." This demonstrates the Spirit's role in enabling people with divine wisdom and ability to accomplish God's work.

Ezekiel 37:1-14 – The Spirit brings life to dry bones: This powerful vision illustrates how the Holy Spirit can revive and restore what seems dead or hopeless. It shows the transformative power of the Spirit in bringing spiritual renewal.

Judges 3:10; 6:34 – The Spirit of the Lord comes upon individuals to empower them for leadership and deliverance: "And the Spirit of the Lord came upon him, and he judged Israel." In these instances, the Spirit of the Lord enabled people like Othniel and Gideon to rise up as leaders and warriors for Israel.

Isaiah 61:1 – A messianic prophecy regarding the Spirit's anointing on Christ: "The Spirit of the Lord God is upon me; because the Lord hath anointed me to preach good tidings unto the meek." This passage speaks directly to the anointing and empowerment of the Messiah, Jesus Christ, through the Holy Spirit.

These references offer a glimpse into the various roles of the Holy Spirit: creator, life-giver, empowerer, and revealer. Through His different manifestations and symbols, we can see how He actively participates in God's plan of creation, redemption, and transformation.

Moving to the New Testament: In Luke 24:49, Jesus speaks of being "endued with power from on high," referring to the promise of the Holy Spirit that would come upon His disciples. The word *endued* means "clothed" or "put on," indicating that believers can be "clothed" with the Spirit. This is a profound and powerful image, signifying that the Holy Spirit doesn't just come alongside us, but envelops us, empowering us for the work God has called us to. This promise marks a pivotal moment in the unfolding of God's plan for His people: the coming of the Holy Spirit to empower believers to carry out the work of the Kingdom.

As we move forward in our study, it is essential to understand that the Holy Spirit, throughout both the Old and New Testaments, is not merely a force or abstract concept but the very presence of God, actively working to guide, empower, and transform believers. The Holy Spirit is central to our experience of God, both in the individual believer's life and in the collective life of the Church.

The Scriptures make it clear that the Holy Spirit's movement is not confined to any single time or place but continues to flow freely, offering renewal, empowerment, and guidance to all who believe. Therefore, understanding the flow of the Spirit as seen through the pages of the Bible will help us better recognize His work in our lives today.

The Holy Ghost or Spirit of the Lord is Fire
(Lev 9:24, 1 Kings 18:38-39, Heb 12:29, Matt 3:11)

The Spirit is often described as fire. This imagery appears in various passages, such as the fire that descended from Heaven in 1 Kings 18:38-39, and in Hebrews 12:29 where our God is described as a consuming fire. Fire not only burns but also provides warmth and light, just as the Holy Ghost purifies us, consuming what does not serve God and empowering us to shine His light to others.

The Spirit is also symbolized as oil for anointing—oil in the Tabernacle's lamp stand kept the fire burning, and both Saul and David were anointed with oil by the prophet, marking them as chosen. In addition, water is another common symbol of the Holy Spirit. Isaiah 12:3 speaks of "water from the wells of salvation," and Ezekiel 36:25 refers to sprinkling clean water upon us. Water symbolizes purification, renewal, and refreshment, much like the Holy Spirit's work in our lives.

The Spirit's movement can be understood through the writings of John and Ezekiel. I hope this provides deeper insight into the Holy Spirit.

The Gospel of John and the Holy Spirit

We will begin with the Gospel of John, building upon our earlier discussion from the book of Acts regarding being filled, being full, and working in the Holy Spirit.

In John 1:32-33, John the Baptist, the forerunner of Christ, testifies that he saw the Spirit descend upon Jesus like a dove. This passage draws from Old Testament references found in Isaiah 42:1 and Isaiah 66:1, which also describe the Spirit of God upon the Messiah. John then affirms that this is the Christ who will baptize with the Holy Ghost.

This is significant because baptism refers to full immersion, not a mere surface experience or a moment of excitement. John is not speaking of a quick prayer or emotional response, but a total immersion into the Holy Spirit. This idea correlates with other passages like **Matthew 3:11**,

Mark 1:8, **Luke 3:16**, and **Acts 1:5**. In **John 3**, Jesus speaks of being "born from above," which is another reference to receiving the Holy Spirit.

The symbolism of fire in these Scriptures reminds us that the Holy Spirit, like fire, purifies, consumes, and empowers. As we allow the Spirit to fill us, we are transformed, and the fire of God burns away impurities, allowing us to live with greater purpose and light.

Importantly, it is **Jesus** who baptizes us with the Holy Ghost. No preacher or individual can give this to us. It is a unique experience from above, similar to standing beneath a waterfall, completely immersed in the Spirit.

John 3:1-8: The New Birth and Spirit Baptism

In **John 3:1-8**, Nicodemus, a Pharisee, comes to Jesus at night. He acknowledges that Jesus is from God. Jesus responds with the declaration that "except a man be born again, he cannot see the kingdom of God." Nicodemus misunderstands, asking how one can be born again, and Jesus clarifies in **verse 5** that "except a man be born of water and of the Spirit, he cannot enter into the kingdom of God."

Let me take a moment to explain these verses. The word "again" in **verse 3** means "from above," referring to a heavenly experience, a divine birth that cannot be fully explained but is a gift from God. Paul in **1 Corinthians 15:22-23** highlights the contrast between Adam's fall, which brought death, and Christ, who through the resurrection brings life. This life-giving Spirit comes from above because Christ is the Spirit Baptizer.

The mention of water and Spirit in Scripture is central to understanding the new birth, as described in Mark 16:15-17, Matthew 28:18-20, and Acts 1:5, which emphasize baptism by immersion. While these passages focus on water baptism, the primary topic I want to address is the baptism of the Spirit, which is essential for entering the kingdom of God. Jesus, though sinless, was baptized to fulfill all righteousness, demonstrating the importance of baptism as both a physical act and a spiritual requirement.

Verse 6 contrasts the flesh with the Spirit, a theme Paul also explores in **1 Corinthians 15**, where he describes how we are born in corruption but raised in incorruption through the work of the Spirit. **In verse 8**, the Spirit is symbolized by wind, illustrating how the Spirit moves freely and its effects are felt, even though its full workings remain a mystery.

The Woman at the Well: John 4: The Spirit as Living Water

In **John 4**, Jesus speaks with a Samaritan woman at Jacob's well. While many scholars believe this aligns with the Holy Spirit's work in **Acts**, it's important to note the symbolism in the conversation. Jesus offers her "living water," referencing the Holy Spirit. He explains that anyone who drinks this water will never thirst again, but it will become a spring of water leading to eternal life.

I must pause here to mention that, from my understanding, Jacob never built a well; he built an altar (Genesis 33:19). Often, the altars in our lives eventually become the wells we draw from later. When Jesus speaks to the Samaritan woman, she is surprised because Jews have no dealings with Samaritans.

In **John 7:37-39**, Jesus again invites those who thirst to come to Him for living water. Here we have another reference to water in relation to the Spirit flowing from someone who believes. This passage beautifully illustrates the concepts of death and resurrection. Jesus had to be glorified before the Holy Ghost could be poured out. There is glorification in His death; Jesus mentioned that He must be lifted up, as the serpent on the pole (John 3:14). What was meant to be a curse, He took upon Himself, becoming that curse so that we might live.

He explains that "out of his belly shall flow rivers of living water," referring to the Holy Spirit, which would be given after His glorification. Jesus had to die, ascend, and be glorified for the Holy Spirit to be poured out. We are called to follow this pattern—Jesus instructed us to take up our cross daily and follow Him. We must die to ourselves, be buried with Him in baptism, and then receive the gift of the Holy Ghost to be witnesses. Just as Jesus ascended into heavenly places, we too can be elevated spiritually. Jesus connects this living water to the eternal life that comes from receiving the Holy Spirit. Like a spring that bubbles up within us, the Holy Spirit empowers believers to live a life of purpose and light.

John 14-16: The Holy Spirit as the Comforter

In **John 14:16-23**, Jesus speaks of sending another Comforter, the Holy Spirit, who will dwell with us and in us. The Comforter, or Advocate, will teach us and remind us of all that Jesus has spoken. This passage highlights the centrality of Jesus in the Holy Spirit's work. Everything the Holy Spirit does is to glorify Jesus.

These texts, referring to the Holy Ghost, promises that the Spirit ensures that we are not left as orphans. Jesus says that although we do not see Him, we know Him because He dwells with us. He also mentions that everything is done in His name (verse 14), and in verse 26, He speaks of the Holy Ghost being sent in His name. All that the Father has revealed in Christ can be manifested in us through the Holy Ghost.

It is in the name of Jesus that we baptize, cast out devils, pray for healing, deliverance, and salvation. The reason for this is that Jesus is the image of the Father (John 14:9) and represents His Father's name (John 5:43). As our Spirit baptizer, He sends the Comforter, as we have clearly seen. The Spirit moves in the name of Jesus.

Philip then asks to see the Father, to which Jesus responds that He is the image of the Father—if you have seen Him, you have seen the Father. This correlates with other scriptures such as Colossians 1:19, 2:9, and Hebrews 1:3, which affirm that Jesus is the image of the invisible God. This image has existed since the foundation of the world, according to God's foreknowledge (Romans 8:29, Genesis 1:26-27, Ezekiel 1:26).

In **John 16:7-15**, Jesus explains that the Holy Spirit will convict the world of sin, righteousness, and judgment, but He will also guide believers into all truth. The Holy Spirit's role is not to speak of Himself but to testify of Christ, furthering the glory of God through His work.

Luke: The Spirit's Work in Action

Luke's writings in both **Luke** and **Acts** provide a unique perspective on the Holy Spirit. In **Luke 4:1, 14**, Jesus, full of the Holy Ghost, is led by the Spirit into the wilderness, and later, He returns in the power of the Spirit. **Luke 10:17-19** is another key passage where Jesus gives authority to His disciples, and they return rejoicing that even demons are subject to His name.

In **Luke 10:19**, Jesus declares, "I give you power to tread on serpents, scorpions, and all the power of the enemy." The authority over spiritual forces reflects the power believers have through the Holy Spirit.

Ezekiel: The Spirit's Work and Prophetic Movement

In the book of **Ezekiel**, the Spirit plays a central role in guiding and empowering the prophet. In **Ezekiel 1:12-20**, the Spirit leads angelic beings who move in perfect alignment with God's will. This demonstrates the forward motion of the

Spirit, always advancing and guiding God's people. Throughout the book, the Spirit is seen taking Ezekiel up and moving him in visions, often lifting him between heaven and earth, paralleling the rapture-like experiences seen in the New Testament.

In **Ezekiel 37:1-14**, the Spirit is seen bringing life to dry bones, symbolizing Israel's spiritual revival. Just as the Spirit breathed life into the dry bones, so too does He breathe life into us, reviving our dead spirits and calling us to eternal life.

The Holy Spirit is the active presence of God in our lives, moving, guiding, empowering, and filling us. He works through fire, water, oil, and breath, leading us into a deeper relationship with God. The Spirit is essential to our salvation, our transformation, and our ability to live out the mission Christ has given us.

Prayerfully, I hope we are beginning to see a common theme regarding the Spirit of God, which can be understood as God in action. This is why, we affirm that God is the Father in creation, the Son in redemption, and the Holy Spirit in regeneration. God knows how to be Father, Son, and Spirit simultaneously without ceasing to be God. I bring this up because Scripture consistently records that when God chooses to move, the actions and terminology used to describe the Spirit's movement remain consistent throughout both the Old and New Testaments.

It's just like how we once were: lost and in chaos. Then the Spirit of God moved upon us, spoke into us, and as we chose to repent and die to our old selves, God, in His mercy, forgave us and filled us with the Holy Ghost, breathing new life into us. We were dead in the first Adam, but made alive in the last Adam.

As we continue through the next two chapters, we begin to explore the main message of this book. I felt it was important to provide an understanding of the Spirit of God in various contexts because often, we are driven by hype, emotions, or a lack of understanding. We need to recognize that true deliverance from our wounds comes when we allow the Spirit to work in ways that only it knows how—through movement and activity in our lives. After the excitement of church services fades, and after the revival moments pass, how do we handle the private times—at home, in our cars, with family, and among friends? Prayerfully, these next chapters will help us explore those wounds and allow the Spirit to heal and set us free.

David Hurst

Grace for the Wounded

Wounds are something we all accumulate in life. As a child, I was very active in sports, running around outside and enjoying life. With that came various injuries, scars, and bruises. Some of my friends, like my brother, even suffered broken bones and needed stitches. I was fortunate enough not to have broken any bones, and I only remember needing stitches once.

One thing we were always told as kids was not to pick at our scabs, scratch our wounds, or mess with any rashes we got. Why? Because it could make things worse, delay healing, and cause more harm than good. Instead, we were advised to clean the wounds with ointment, water, or peroxide, to help the healing process. In the next chapter, we'll delve deeper into the healing process, particularly focusing on water.

Much like our physical wounds, our walk with God can also leave us with spiritual wounds, scars, and injuries. Even after we are saved, we often hold on to past deficiencies, thinking we are not good enough. We may continue picking at old wounds and scars, allowing them to hinder our growth and healing.

Leviticus 21:17-23 provides an interesting perspective on this. Let's take a look at these verses:

Leviticus 21:17-23 (KJV): 17 "Speak unto Aaron, saying, Whosoever he be of thy seed in their generations that hath any blemish, let him not approach to offer the bread of his God.
18 For whatsoever man he be that hath a blemish, he shall not approach: a blind man, or a lame, or he that hath a flat nose, or anything superfluous,
19 Or a man that is broken-footed, or broken-handed,
20 Or crook-backed, or a dwarf, or that hath a

blemish in his eye, or be scurvy, or scabbed, or hath his stones broken;

21 No man that hath a blemish of the seed of Aaron the priest shall come nigh to offer the offerings of the Lord made by fire: he hath a blemish; he shall not come nigh to offer the bread of his God.

22 He shall eat the bread of his God, both of the most holy and of the holy.

23 Only he shall not go in unto the veil, nor come nigh unto the altar, because he hath a blemish; that he profane not my sanctuaries: for I the Lord do sanctify them."

Leviticus is often considered a challenging book to understand, especially with its focus on the Levites and the priesthood. Many consider it one of the most difficult books to study and learn from. However, there are some points to keep in mind that can help us grasp its meaning:

- Leviticus primarily focuses on holiness and consecration, and it mentions the term "holy" over 90 times.
- In the Old Covenant, only certain individuals—specifically the priests—were

allowed to approach God in the Holy of Holies. Under the New Covenant, we are now all called to be priests (1 Peter 2:9), with Jesus as our High Priest.

- Exodus (the book before Leviticus) deals with redemption, while Leviticus speaks of our ongoing walk with God after we are redeemed.

One key thing to remember is that the book of Leviticus is deeply centered on God's holiness. The Lord is holy, and He calls His people to be holy as well (Leviticus 11:44). As we examine the passage above, we see that the priests, who were to be sanctified for service to God, were restricted from coming close to God's presence if they had any physical deformity. They could eat the bread, but they could not approach the altar or enter the veil because they had blemishes. This limitation, though seemingly harsh, emphasizes the holiness of God and the importance of sanctification.

Now, let's look at the physical flaws mentioned in Leviticus 21:17-23 and explore their spiritual meanings:

1. **Blindness** – The priest had to see the things of God to serve properly. Spiritually, we need to be able to perceive God's truth or we risk being spiritually blind.

2. **Lameness** – The priest had to be able to walk and function in his priestly role. Similarly, we must be able to walk according to the Word of God and not be spiritually lame.

3. **Flat Nose** – Spiritually, this could symbolize gossip, backbiting, or hating others. When we allow these behaviors, we distort the image of God in us.

4. **Superfluous (Excessive)** – Anything in excess, such as pride or arrogance, is harmful to our spiritual walk.

5. **Broken Hand or Foot** – The priest had to be able to work. Spiritually, we must be able to serve and function according to God's plan.

6. **Crooked Back** – This symbolizes integrity. We should stand upright and not allow the crookedness of the world to bend us.

7. **Blemish in the Eye** – This could refer to lust of the eyes. Allowing lust to take root in our hearts will ultimately lead to spiritual blindness.

8. **Scurvy or Scabs** – Scurvy often results from poor diet, while scabs indicate wounds that are still healing. Spiritually, we must ensure we are feeding our souls with the right things, and we need to allow God to heal our wounds and scars.

9. **Dwarf** – This could represent a lack of spiritual strength or maturity. We must grow strong in our faith and not remain weak.

10. **Broken Stones (Emasculated)** – This could represent men feeling emasculated, especially in today's society. God calls men to be strong, biblical leaders in their homes and communities.

So, if you feel weak, inadequate, or unable to approach a holy God due to your imperfections, know that you are not alone. Many of us feel this way at times. However, God does not call us to approach Him based on our own merit or holiness. Verse 23 of Leviticus 21 reminds us that God sanctifies those He calls. We cannot sanctify ourselves; it is God's work to make us holy.

The reason for such strict standards for priests is similar to the strict standards for selecting the sacrifice for the atonement offering, just as each piece of the tabernacle was very specific. In Hebrews, it speaks of Moses recording what he saw, and how we now have a more perfect tabernacle. The blood of bulls and goats could not save us, but there was one who could. Now, we have a high priest in heavenly places.

When we consider that the lamb needed to be without blemish and that the tabernacle represented Christ, it becomes clear why the priests also had to be without blemish. The priests had to represent Christ in that role. While Christ was without sin, He could still suffer wounds and bleed, as we saw during the crucifixion. He may have even developed calluses from His work, just as the priests of the Old Testament likely endured small cuts and wounds. Christ, as the perfect representation of the priest, was part of a greater priesthood, after the order of Melchizedek—an unchangeable priesthood (Hebrews 7:23-28). He was able to enter into the holy of holies not made with human hands (Hebrews 9:22).

When Christ, our Messiah, died on the cross, the veil of the temple was torn from top to bottom, allowing us to commune directly with a holy God. He is our mediator between God and man. We, too, should allow ourselves to be rent—from head to toe—so that we can be open to a holy God. Just as Christ is the first fruits of the resurrection of the dead (1 Corinthians 15:20), the Lamb slain from the foundation of the world (Revelation 13:8), and the Lamb who takes away the sins of the world, as John the Baptist declared, we see that Christ fulfilled the priestly role in a perfect and complete way.

Christ fulfilled the law (Matthew 5:17). Therefore, at the end of Leviticus, the Lord sanctifies them, and since Christ is now our high priest, and the veil was rent from top to bottom, we—despite our deficiencies—have access to a holy God.

This idea is expanded in the New Testament. Hebrews 4:14-16 reminds us that we can approach God boldly because we have a High Priest—Jesus—who understands our weaknesses and infirmities. He was tempted in every way we are, yet without sin. We can come to Him and receive mercy and grace in our time of need.

Hebrews 4:14-16 (KJV):
14 "Seeing then that we have a great high priest, that is passed into the heavens, Jesus the Son of God, let us hold fast our profession.
15 For we have not an high priest which cannot be touched with the feeling of our infirmities; but was in all points tempted like as we are, yet without sin.
16 Let us therefore come boldly unto the throne of grace, that we may obtain mercy, and find grace to help in time of need."

You see that? We can have access to a holy God through Jesus. He understands all our infirmities, wounds, and scars. He became and took on all that for us so that we might be able to come to Him. What was lost because of the fall of Adam is redeemed by the Last Adam. Only Christ could sanctify us.

What did Jesus do many times in His earthly ministry? He opened blinded eyes, healed withered hands, made the lame walk, caused the issue of blood to dry up, healed the leper, and healed a woman with a crooked back for 18 years. Many of these issues Jesus healed were the same issues mentioned in Leviticus 21.

I can't make this up! I am rejoicing while writing this because I know God can take the issues we have been plagued with for years, and because of what Jesus did, He can bring us to a holy God, to His throne of grace, where we can find healing.

Now, let's address the questions posed earlier. I feel deficient, weak, and unable to do anything. How can I approach a holy God after all that? I don't ever feel truly holy. Am I good enough?

The answer is this: We may feel deficient or weak, but the Bible declares that in our weakness, He is made strong (2 Corinthians 12:9-10). As for being good enough or holy, the Bible says our righteousness is as filthy rags before the Lord, and that it is only God who can impute righteousness and holiness into us (Isaiah 64:6, Romans 4:22).

I believe this makes Isaiah 53 much more powerful. "He was wounded for our transgressions, and bruised for our iniquities." Transgression refers to rebellion, while iniquity represents perversity, depravity, and guilt. Griefs in the text refers to anxieties and calamities, while sorrows represent pains. This is the arm of the Lord revealed: He took all that upon Himself so that we might come to Him. The scripture also says that the arm of the Lord is not too short to save. The Lord Jesus knows how to fully heal us and deliver us.

Many believers continue to struggle with things that afflict their soul and body, unable to lay them on the altar and truly confess them. Speaking of confession, we can learn much from King David in the Bible. He was a man willing to confess and open up to the Lord. When the prophet called him out for his affair and murder, he repented. When he knew he had messed up and numbered the people, he repented again.

Psalm 32:1-5 is a powerful scripture that shows how David understood forgiveness, covering, and confession. I believe the same is true for us. We allow the sins of the past, and issues we've had in our walk with God, to hinder us from going to the throne of grace. God doesn't want us to just hold these things in; He desires us to be open with Him. When we do that, He will begin to work in our lives, heal us, and make us new creatures in Christ, molded by His hand.

This leads to true holiness in our walk with God. As I mentioned earlier, many times we do well with covering up and looking the part, yet internally we are bleeding out. Instead of dealing with the issue, we cover it up. Sometimes we think our outward appearance will protect us, or we idolize the outward appearance to such an extent that it becomes an idol. That said, I do fully believe in outward holiness and separation, presenting ourselves in a Christlike manner. I am not bashing our standards but praying that we truly return to examining the inside. I believe that from covering Adam and Eve in the garden to the priests and onward, modesty is expected as we grow in our walk with God.

Jesus spoke often about how the outward appearance could look good, but the inside could be dead, or how it's the inner person that truly defiles a man (Matthew 15:1-20, Matthew 23:1-5 and 23-28). Something I observed recently, during back-to-back storms in my area, was how some huge trees were uprooted or broken in parts, revealing that they were hollow inside, or their roots were not deep. The Hurricane Milton winds were strong, and I think the full aftermath is yet to be determined. Often, something that appears strong outwardly or immovable may have shallow roots and be hollow inside.

This can happen to us as believers, or to those we have been hurt by in the past—those we thought were strong and immovable. But over time, issues eat away at the inside, and the roots don't grow deep. Eventually, things happen, and the outward appearance proves that what looked strong was dead inside, just as Jesus described in some of His teachings. Sometimes storms or issues come so God can uproot the shallow things in our lives that aren't needed, or to show us that certain things are dead and need to go.

Why am I saying this? Well, when we have scars, wounds, and deficiencies that affect us daily, eventually we may allow the inside to show, regardless of how much we cover it up with outward appearances. Eventually, blood, when hemorrhaging, will bleed through the cloth. The Bible says, "Out of the abundance of the heart, the mouth speaks." The issues I want to help believers deal with—and what has helped me in my walk with God—are issues of the heart. If we can allow ourselves to be in the hands of a holy God and allow Him to mold us, He is the potter (Jeremiah 18), and David knew that even in judgment and correction, there is mercy when we are in the hands of God (2 Samuel 24:14).

True confession should be made to the Lord, realizing that in this walk to the end, it is the Lord who sanctifies us. In my experience, this has worked for me in battling anger, competitiveness, jealousy, unforgiveness, and perversion. It took years for some of these things to be delivered from me. In the past, I would gloss over them, thinking they were just things that happen, and telling myself, "God knows my heart." But I didn't realize until years later that these struggles truly affected my mental health and how I treated people.

Now, the struggles are not as intense. Are they attacks from the enemy? Sure, but that's because the enemy doesn't want me walking with God.

Over the last four years, since my wake-up call during COVID, I have asked God to search me— not only to search me, but to mold and shape me into the image He desires me to be. With that process comes the squeezing out of past issues, and things that I thought were buried begin to rise. Don't fret over it—it's part of the healing process. Just as gold is refined by fire, the impurities rise to the top and are cleaned away, leaving pure gold. Similarly, God wants to purify us by allowing these impurities to rise so they can be removed. As Peter said, we will come out as pure gold.

In that process, I learned to be honest in prayer. I've confessed, "I felt like punching someone in the face today," or "I was jealous or envious of someone," or "Impure thoughts of old times that I haven't thought of in years came to mind." I immediately go to repentance and denounce these attacks, thinking on the Lord. Why? Because I have a throne of grace I can go to, and I can let God know what's bothering me.

You will begin to see fruit from God because, as old things are uprooted, new things are planted. Over time, you'll see the deliverance process in your life, where the old appetites no longer exist, and a God-given thirst for Him grows deeper. With that said, farming analogies are often used in Scripture, referring to seed, planting, and harvest.

Much of what happens to us is deeply rooted in us—even after we are filled with the Holy Ghost. There are things from our past that can still be deeply rooted inside us. It takes time to get to the root cause. The Holy Ghost, our teacher, helps reveal these things so God can uproot them and plant fresh new seed. This process is called cultivating—turning the hard soil to make it good for planting. We are made from the dust of the earth, and the Word of God is seed. We need to be good soil, willing to be cultivated, so the Word can grow within us. This all deals with deep things—heart issues, dark corners we may have allowed ourselves to forget, and God is trying to remind us so He can heal our hurts.

Finally, let's reference the tabernacle. When we look at the tabernacle of Moses, the first instructions were regarding the Ark of the Covenant. Following the tabernacle plan, we start from the outside and work inward. But with God, He starts inward, with the Ark of the Covenant, and works outward. The Ark of the Covenant was to hold the tables of stone on the inside, where the mercy seat sat. This shows us that inside the Holy of Holies, there was mercy above the law, if the blood was applied. God will have mercy within us if we are willing to approach Him. And as He works within us, the fruit of His work will be seen on the outside, not some fake or phony form of godliness.

When approaching God, we start with the biggest piece of furniture in the tabernacle: the altar of sacrifice. This should be the biggest part of our personal lives as well—being a willing sacrifice to God, allowing death to ourselves while He does His work. The altar was not to be altered or manipulated, because many times people would worship the work of their hands rather than God. We try to prove our work in this area, but God says the work is His.

Moving past the laver of water—a type of washing and cleansing—death brings blood, and there is a washing away by water. There are three pieces of furniture I found interesting:

- The cherubim on the mercy seat—were to be a beaten work (Exodus 25:18).
- The golden candlestick—was to be a beaten work (Exodus 25:31).
- Olive oil for the lamp—was to be beaten for the light (Exodus 27:20).

As we approach God, we notice these items are beaten. This is significant because it speaks to light and anointing. The light of God will form, mold, and shape us. Sometimes it's painful, sometimes we wonder why there is pressure—

but it's God forming us. Jesus said we are the light of the world. The light must shine through something—it cannot be a closed container. There has to be a breaking forth, and only God can truly do that.

As we close this chapter, we see that much can be said about our wounds, scars, and our walk with God in holiness. We must not simply cover ourselves. Too often, we forget to take off the armor of God and find rest and intimacy in His presence. There are six days to work and labor, but on the seventh, God does what only He can do. As we move to the next chapter, let this be a time where you allow God to enter into the places you've buried. There is true rest and intimacy with God, where only He can provide the healing, molding, and shaping needed for us to become the vessels He desires us to be.

Wells of Deliverance

My belief after the last chapter is that things finally clicked, and you can start to experience relief knowing that you can bring your infirmities and issues to God. Let's continue down this path by examining Ezekiel 47, breaking down the scriptures and connecting them to Spirit baptism, the moving of the Spirit, and healing.

Ezekiel 47 is part of the vision he receives of the kingdom after the tribulation, where he sees the new temple and what it represents. This vision spans Ezekiel 40–48, which speaks about the new Jerusalem and the tabernacle. Chapter 47 is a powerful section of scripture to study, and we can already see prophetic fulfillment happening in verses 8-10. If you remember earlier in the book, where Spirit baptism and the movement of the Spirit are discussed in both John and Ezekiel, you'll notice that water is referenced often in this chapter. Keep in mind that water in the Bible is often symbolic of the Spirit, as Jesus mentioned in John.

Let's look at Ezekiel 47:1-10, with verses 11 and 12 also being valuable for further study on your own:

Ezekiel 47:1-10 (KJV):

1. Afterward he brought me again unto the door of the house; and, behold, waters issued out from under the threshold of the house eastward: for the forefront of the house stood toward the east, and the waters came down from under the right side of the house, at the south side of the altar.
2. Then brought he me out of the way of the gate northward, and led me about the way without unto the utter gate by the way that looketh eastward; and, behold, there ran out waters on the right side.

3. And when the man that had the line in his hand went forth eastward, he measured a thousand cubits, and he brought me through the waters; the waters were to the ankles.

4. Again he measured a thousand, and brought me through the waters; the waters were to the knees. Again he measured a thousand, and brought me through; the waters were to the loins.

5. Afterward he measured a thousand; and it was a river that I could not pass over: for the waters were risen, waters to swim in, a river that could not be passed over.

6. And he said unto me, Son of man, hast thou seen this? Then he brought me, and caused me to return to the brink of the river.

7. Now when I had returned, behold, at the bank of the river were very many trees on the one side and on the other.

8. Then said he unto me, These waters issue out toward the east country, and go down into the desert, and go into the sea:

which being brought forth into the sea, the waters shall be healed.

9. And it shall come to pass, that everything that liveth, which moveth, whithersoever the rivers shall come, shall live: and there shall be a very great multitude of fish, because these waters shall come thither: for they shall be healed; and everything shall live whither the river cometh.

10. And it shall come to pass, that the fishers shall stand upon it from Engedi even unto Eneglaim; they shall be a place to spread forth nets; their fish shall be according to their kinds, as the fish of the great sea, exceeding man.

In verse 1, Ezekiel is brought to the door of the tabernacle and sees water flowing from the threshold of the house. The threshold, in biblical terms, is the bottom of the doorway, which often keeps the elements out. It represents a type of barrier.

What threshold or barrier is preventing us from being fully immersed in the Spirit of God? Jesus stated that we would have wells springing up with living water, rivers of living water flowing from us. Whether or not we have been baptized in the Spirit, many of us still have a threshold stopping that flow.

In verse 3, Ezekiel is measured with waters reaching his ankles. Many of us experience this in our walk with the Spirit—just dipping our toes in, feeling the Spirit's presence, but still controlling the situation. We sense the movement at times, but we still hold onto so much control. This "ankle-deep" spiritual walk may not be wrong, but we often find ourselves subject to our thoughts, flesh, and emotions. We show up to services, get our "fix," and leave with little change.

As Paul mentions, there is a difference between being a babe in Christ and a mature adult in Christ. Our walk should progress. We may still face trouble and challenges, but there should be growth and maturity in the Spirit.

In verse 4, the water reaches Ezekiel's knees, representing the next level of immersion. At this stage, there is still some control, but you're taking steps of faith. As the water reaches his loins (verse 5), Ezekiel begins to lose control, and the Spirit moves him, pushing him deeper.

This is significant: when the Spirit nudges you, it may feel like you're being knocked off balance — God won't let you fall. He's gently guiding you into deeper trust in Him, a trust that everything in the natural may seem chaotic, but in the Spirit, you are carried and held.

In **verse 5**, the waters rise to the point where Ezekiel is fully immersed—a river that he cannot cross. This is the immersion into the Spirit. It's a full baptism, something we see referenced in Acts and by Jesus and John the Baptist. This immersion isn't about constant spiritual highs or feeling euphoric all the time, but rather about a deep reliance on the Holy Spirit. Even when things feel out of control, we can rest in the Spirit, knowing that God is in control and will work everything out.

In **verses 6-7**, Ezekiel is brought back to the brink of the river, where many trees line both sides of the water. In the Bible, trees often represent people. Jeremiah 17:7-8 tells us that those who trust the Lord are like trees planted by water, yielding fruit. Jesus, in John 15, also describes Himself as the vine and us as the branches. Isaiah 61:3 calls us "trees of righteousness, the planting of the Lord."

Being planted and rooted in Christ is essential. As we stay connected to Him, the flow of the Spirit will bring forth fruit. Our spiritual roots will grow deep, and God will be glorified in us.

Verses 8-9 speak of the waters healing the sea and bringing life wherever they flow. When the river touches the desert or the dead sea, everything it touches is healed and made alive.

It's important to pause here and reflect: The river is flowing to the Dead Sea, and where it flows, it heals. Rivers are essential for life, both physically and spiritually. As National Geographic calls rivers the "veins of the Earth," they are life-giving forces, just as the Spirit is a life-giving force in our spiritual lives.

Water is necessary for physical life—whether it's hydration, cleaning, or healing wounds.

Spiritually, the same applies. If we allow the movement of the Spirit in our lives, it can heal our spiritual wounds, deliver us from burdens, and bring new life to dead things. The key is to let the Spirit flow through us, rather than just stopping at us, which would cause spiritual stagnation.

Rivers are a source of life, while stagnant waters, like those of the Dead Sea, represent death. Jesus desires life to flow through us, not just to us. When we receive life from God, it should flow through us to others.

Here are some examples of rivers in the Bible:

- The Garden of Eden had four rivers.
- Joshua and Israel crossed the Jordan River before entering the Promised Land.
- Elijah and Elisha crossed the Jordan River.
- Naaman dipped seven times in the Jordan River and was healed.
- Jesus Himself was baptized in the Jordan River as an example.

Finally, Ezekiel sees water flowing from the tabernacle, and since we are considered the tabernacle of the Holy Spirit, I believe we need more of this flowing Spirit in these last days. As rivers of living water flow in us, they bring healing, peace, and rest.

The Bible tells us that "the joy of the Lord is my strength." How do we receive joy? In His presence, where there is fullness of joy. By being vulnerable in the presence of God, allowing Him to work on those deep wounds, we can experience the flow of living water in us and through us.

My desire for this chapter is that we would be willing to be fully vulnerable in God's presence, allowing the Spirit to heal past wounds and deficiencies. Jesus spoke of forgiveness and healing all infirmities. Whatever you've dealt with—whether it's pride, addiction, or emotional pain—bring it to the feet of the One who baptizes us with the Holy Ghost. As we come to Him daily, He will take away our burdens, fill us with His Spirit, and help us bear fruit for His kingdom. When life flows through us, that life-giving Spirit will draw others to Jesus through us.

Mended While Ministering

This chapter may seem out of place or strange to some. You may be asking, "How can I be healed while helping others find healing?" Throughout this book, you may recall much talk about rivers—about flowing, movement, and, as Ezekiel 47 mentions, life that happens by the rivers. When we think of rivers, we often focus not only on the life outside the river, but also on the life that exists within the flowing waters.

There's much we can learn from rivers that applies to this topic. Let me point out a few key insights from my study and research:

- **Rivers flow from an elevated plain:** The higher the elevation, the more powerful the stream flows downward. Biblically, we have no higher elevation than a baptism from a heavenly source.

- **Rivers flow downward through gravity:** There's a pulling of the Spirit that moves us deeper and allows the things of God to work through many of us.
- **Rivers are fed by tributaries:** A tributary is a stream that flows into a larger body of water. It can also mean an entity or individual that contributes to a greater cause, providing aid or support.

Let's dwell on this for a moment. Some of these meanings point to a form of agreement, tribute, or aid contributing to something larger. Paul said that we are the body of Christ, each of us having a specific purpose. In the kingdom of God, there's something we can all contribute.

However, when we talk about unity in the church, especially within the apostolic tradition, we often focus only on unity within our own organization or denomination. We forget that we all have a part to play in the bigger picture of true apostolic unity.

If one group plants, and another waters, it is God who gives the increase. This truth applies whether we're part of the Pentecostal Assemblies of the World or the United Pentecostal Church, or other Spirit-filled Pentecostal groups.

I will go a step further: if the Church of God in Christ, the Church of God, or the Assemblies of God planted, and the Assemblies of the Lord Jesus Christ or another charismatic group watered, was it not still God who gave the increase? My point is this: too often the Spirit is moving and calling, regardless of denominations, and many times we miss it because it doesn't fit within our organization's standards. Just as a river is fed by many tributaries, the flow of the Spirit is nourished by different streams. Let us be willing to catch hold of it and become part of the Spirit-filled, end-time church. We should remember that the Spirit moves across all boundaries, and we must be open to contributing to the broader work of the Spirit-filled church.

The next point about rivers is the **banks** of the river. Water is a powerful force. It erodes rocks and leaves imprints in the earth. The Grand Canyon, for example, is believed to have been formed by the Colorado River over many years. If we, as the dust of the earth, allow the Spirit (symbolized by rivers of living water) to flow through us, we, too, can be shaped and formed over time.

Sometimes, when we feel beaten and moved in a direction we didn't expect, we may not realize that the Spirit is shaping our path, much like a river carves out its course over years. The pressure, pushing, and moving we feel is the Spirit's work in forming us.

The river eventually ends in a much larger body of water, and this symbolizes our end goal—our heavenly home. As we flow in the Spirit, we are all striving toward this ultimate destination.

Healing Through the Spirit: A Flow That Heals and Transforms

As we find healing in the Spirit, we begin to discover that God knows how to heal us and mold us. At the same time, the Spirit leads us to help others fulfill God's purpose in their lives. Paul reminds us in 1 Corinthians 6:11 that we are washed, sanctified, and justified in the name of the Lord Jesus, by the Spirit of our God.

Often, we forget where we came from as believers and the importance of the Great Commission. Jesus commanded us to go into all the world, teaching and baptizing in the name of the Father, Son, and Holy Ghost. Reaching out, making disciples, and baptizing people in Jesus' name is crucial to our walk with God.

It's essential to understand that we are never saved by our works. Our earthly fathers give good gifts to their children, as described in Scripture. 1 Corinthians 13 speaks of bestowing goods to the poor, but without charity or love, it profits nothing. The Bible emphasizes faith in God and helping others through Godly love. We are called to bring the kingdom of God to others, being His hands and feet on earth (1 Corinthians 13, Luke 10:9-11, Matthew 25:31-46).

Let's reflect on Isaiah 58:5-12, which speaks about true fasting and helping others. While many use this chapter to describe the practice of fasting, it encompasses much more. God reveals that fasting is not just about breaking chains and tearing down strongholds; it also involves helping those in need. This passage shows that when we genuinely serve others, our light will shine, our health will be restored, and healing will take place.

The Ten Commandments serve as an important reminder of this principle. The first four commandments focus on our relationship with God, while the remaining six address our relationship with others. John wrote that if you claim to love God but hate your brother, you are a liar (1 John 4:20). Jesus stated that all the Law and the Prophets are summed up in two commandments: love the Lord your God with all your heart, mind, and soul, and love your neighbor as yourself (Matthew 22:38-40). Jesus quoted this from Leviticus 19:18.

Isaiah 58:7 tells us to share our bread with the hungry, bring the poor into our homes, and clothe the naked. This type of sacrifice is what God desires. When we give, even in small ways—like sacrificing a meal or a cup of coffee—and share with those in need, we become conduits for God's Spirit to flow through us.

When we fast, pray, and seek God's face, we must remember that we are also called to serve others, as Jesus demonstrated. Verse 8 says, "Then shall thy light break forth, and thy health (healing) shall spring forth." When we fast, turn to God, and remember our purpose, we will shine like a light, and healing will follow.

Jesus said that we are the light of the world. There is something powerful about being moved by God to worship Him. When we do, the light will break forth, and healing will take place. Verse 9 emphasizes the importance of a repentant heart—turning away from the past. When we do, God will work in us and heal us.

Verse 10 repeats the call to extend our hearts to the hungry and satisfy the afflicted soul. Then our light will shine in the darkness. God knows how to move in the darkest, most desolate places, when we feel that all hope is lost. When we answer His call, we begin to see light burst forth.

Verses 11-12 promise that the Lord will guide us, make our bones strong, satisfy our souls in dry places, and make us like a watered garden—like a spring of water, whose waters never fail. These waters bring life and substance, renewing us again and again. Wasted places are rebuilt, and paths are restored.

Keep these verses in mind, as I will be going through much scripture. God spoke through the prophet Isaiah, declaring that this type of fast—this walk with Him, this sacrifice of helping others—gets His attention, allowing light to shine in darkness and bringing healing and restoration. There is healing and restoration when we allow the Spirit to move in us and through us to help others in a biblical way.

Throughout the Old Testament, we see that God has consistently desired to be worshiped alone, and in our desire to worship Him, we are called to minister to others as well. The Bible instructs us to do everything in word or deed as if we are doing it unto the Lord (Colossians 3:17). Jesus did not come to destroy the law, but to fulfill it (Matthew 5:17). In the previous verse, Jesus speaks about letting our light shine before others so they can see our good works (Matthew 5:16).

In Deuteronomy 15:1-11, we learn several key principles. The passage begins with the release of debts every seven years, where creditors are not to collect from their fellow Israelites. This is similar to Paul's teaching in 1 Corinthians 6:1-11 about avoiding disputes with fellow believers. While civil matters should be handled with forgiveness and grace, criminal matters are to be left to the courts. Verses 7-11 emphasize not hardening our hearts toward the poor, but instead lending a hand and forgiving debts after seven years. Verse 11 states, "the poor shall never cease out of the land," which Jesus echoes in Matthew 26:11, saying, "The poor you will always have with you."

Thus, God expects us to serve others in our walk with Him, just as He has served us. As Isaiah 58 illustrates, when we truly desire to walk with the Lord and love Him, He begins a work in us. This work is not for fame or glory, but for the advancement of God's kingdom and walking in the Spirit.

Exodus 23:1-9 echoes similar themes, warning against bearing false witness, perverting justice (verse 1), following the crowd to do evil (verse 2), and urging us to help even our enemies (verse 4). Jesus, in Luke 6:27-35, teaches us to love even those who oppose us, showing that loving those who love us is easy, but showing God's love to our enemies takes more. The passage also warns against taking bribes or oppressing strangers (verses 8-9). Proverbs 11:25 states, "A liberal soul shall be made fat (or rich); he that waters shall be watered himself."

While some may think these principles are not necessary today, let us recall the Great Commission—to reach souls and be ambassadors for Christ. An ambassador represents their country in a foreign land, and as believers, we represent God's kingdom on earth. The question I ask myself and all of us daily is: *Am I representing God's kingdom to others according to Scripture?*

The Bible is clear about believing and going forth, and there are great benefits in working in the harvest field. Ruth, a Gentile, found her husband in the harvest field, which serves as a type of the Gentile bride, and Boaz as a type of Christ, the kinsman redeemer. If we truly want to be close to

Christ as our kinsman redeemer, we must be found in the field, laboring for His kingdom.

Matthew 25:31-46 further emphasizes the importance of ministering to others. Jesus said that whatever we do for the least of these, we do for Him. There is a separation of the sheep and the goats. We are not saved by works, but our actions should reflect God's love and bring healing to others. God is serious about how we serve in the kingdom, and our service should be motivated by love, not for self-glory, but for His kingdom.

Through **Galatians 6:1-9**, we are encouraged to bear one another's burdens and restore those who have fallen. In our walk with God, we should be quick to show mercy and forgiveness, just as Jesus did for those who betrayed Him. It's essential to lift others up and encourage their return to God, as we all have experienced brokenness at some point.

So how can we help others, even without giving them material things? We can offer the same mercy and forgiveness that Jesus extended to those who betrayed and killed Him. Matthew

18:12-35 provides great insight for this study. It begins with the parable of the lost sheep, emphasizing the importance of seeking out those who are lost. The chapter then transitions into a teaching on forgiveness, with verses 15-22 in between discussing binding and loosing—concepts closely tied to our ability to forgive. Our power to bind and loose is directly related to our capacity to forgive. Just look at Jesus on the Cross—after He forgave, great things happened. Similarly, when Stephen forgave those who stoned him, Paul was converted.

Another example is found in Galatians 6:1, where we are called to help others return to the Lord, restoring and edifying those who have fallen. Often, our problem is that when people make mistakes, we tend to belittle them. While proper correction is necessary—just as Paul and Jesus did—it must be accompanied by mercy. The reason many backsliders don't return to the house of the Lord is that while they know the Father will forgive them, they fear rejection from the church. The story of the prodigal son illustrates this beautifully, showing how the father welcomed his son back with open arms, while others may have judged him.

The Flow of Living Waters: A Daily Journey

In my experience, when we desire to be in God's will, He often places people in our paths who need a word or help we can provide. The Bible teaches that we are overcomers by the blood of the Lamb and the word of our testimony (Revelation 12:11). Sharing our experiences brings healing not only to others but also to ourselves.

It's through the flowing of living waters—the Spirit—that we experience healing. We become edified, comforted, and strengthened, not just during Sunday services, but throughout the week. The Spirit allows us to grow and bear fruit, just like any plant requires water to thrive.

Taking up our cross daily (Luke 9:23) is a part of our journey with Christ. It requires dying to self every day. As we genuinely seek healing and wholeness, we come before a holy God, surrendering ourselves, and in doing so, God leads us to others who either need the same help or have overcome similar struggles—because iron sharpens iron. This process is truly a baptism of the Spirit, a daily refreshing in the Holy Ghost, with rivers of living water flowing from above, through us, and to those God directs us to. In this way, we can be healed, delivered, and made whole in Jesus' name.

David Hurst

My Last Sentiments

I want to thank you for taking the time to read this book. I pray that it has been edifying, enlightening, and that you have gained understanding that brings you closer to our Lord Jesus Christ. My prayer is that we, as the end-time church, whether new to the faith or seasoned believers, experience healing and refreshing in the Spirit. The baptism of the Holy Ghost is more than a one-time experience. As Paul wrote in 1 Corinthians 14, those who speak in tongues edify themselves and speak mysteries unto God.

When we allow ourselves to be vulnerable in His presence, the Spirit moves in us and through us, providing peace, comfort, and healing. The healing process may be long, as some issues in our lives are deeply rooted. But with the help of the Holy Ghost, we can find peace, forgiveness, and deliverance. God is our provider, father, protector, savior, and friend. We have access to the river of life, which heals and restores.

I hope everyone reading this finds true healing through the flow of God's Spirit. As we come to the end of this journey, I want to leave you with a reminder that the process of healing and spiritual growth is ongoing. Just as rivers are constantly flowing and shaping the land, God's Spirit continually moves in us, refining, healing, and directing our paths. No matter where you are in your walk with God, there is always room to grow, always room to heal, and always more of God to experience.

In moments of brokenness, in moments of joy, in moments of uncertainty, the Spirit is there, ready to guide you, fill you, and refresh you. And as you find healing in the Holy Spirit, remember that part of that healing is being able to help heal others. There is power in community, in unity, in being part of the body of Christ, and working together in the Spirit. No one is alone in this journey. As you continue to grow in the knowledge of God's love and power, may you be a vessel of healing to those around you.

Finally, I want to encourage you to stay faithful, stay humble, and never lose sight of the incredible gift of the Holy Ghost. Whether you are a new believer or have been walking with God for years, there is always more to discover, more to experience, and more to give. As we wait for the return of our Lord, let us be rivers of life in a dry and thirsty land, pouring out the healing power of the Holy Spirit to all who need it. May God bless you richly as you continue to seek His presence and walk in His light. **Sincerely,** David Hurst

Key Takeaways

The Holy Spirit is a constant presence that empowers us for daily living.

The Spirit heals, guides, and strengthens us in our walk with God.

The Holy Spirit brings healing to our hearts, minds, and bodies.

Healing involves surrendering our wounds to God and allowing the Spirit to restore us.

Personal Application:
Spend five minutes in prayer, asking the Holy Spirit to reveal areas where you need healing and empowerment. Journal your thoughts and any insights that come to mind.

Interactive Exercise:
Draw or write about a time when you felt empowered by the Holy Spirit. Reflect on how that experience impacted your faith.

Take time for a healing prayer exercise. Sit in quiet prayer, inviting the Holy Spirit to reveal any wounds or emotional burdens you need to release. Pray for healing in those areas.

Scripture to Meditate On:

Isaiah 53:5 – "But he was pierced for our transgressions, he was crushed for our iniquities; the punishment that brought us peace was on him, and by his wounds we are healed."

Questions

Since being Spirit filled, have you emotionally healed?

_____
_____
_____
_____
_____
_____
_____
_____
_____
_____
_____
_____
_____
_____
_____
_____
_____
_____
_____
_____

How do you sense the Holy Spirit Is impacting your prayer life?

_____
_____
_____
_____
_____
_____
_____
_____
_____
_____
_____
_____
_____
_____
_____
_____
_____
_____
_____
_____
_____

What do you cherish about being empowered by the Holy Spirit?

_____

_____

_____

_____

_____

_____

_____

_____

_____

_____

_____

_____

_____

_____

_____

_____

_____

_____

_____

_____

_____

_____

David Hurst

How did you forgive offenses and become spiritually effective after encountering healing?

_____
_____
_____
_____
_____
_____
_____
_____
_____
_____
_____
_____
_____
_____
_____
_____
_____
_____
_____
_____
_____
_____

After reading the book do you see the importance of believers praying in tongues?

_____
_____
_____
_____
_____
_____
_____
_____
_____
_____
_____
_____
_____
_____
_____
_____
_____
_____
_____
_____
_____
_____
_____
_____

David Hurst